My Beloved Dogs

Record Keeping for the Canine Competitor and Multi-Dog Home

My Beloved Dogs • Record Keeping for the Canine Competitor and Multi-Dog Home

copyright © 2015 Leila Grandemange

first printing August, 2015

ISBN 978-0-9826854-7-1

Sunny Ville
PUBLISHING

Table of Contents

 How to Use This Book

My **Beloved Dogs** is a record keeping book for the canine competitor and the multi-dog home. This book was created to help you stay organized. It is unique in that each dog's basic information, breeding, and health history will be recorded right along with its achievements, titles earned, and anything else related to managing a multi-dog home. This makes it the ideal companion to take along to dog shows, the vet, health testing clinics, or anywhere you may need easy access to all your dogs' important information. Going on vacation? Your pet sitter will also appreciate having each dog's health history in hand in case of emergency. The book is divided into three main parts:

PART I: Quick reference of your dogs, hopeful pups, heat cycles, and stud service

PART II: Detailed information about each dog

PART III: Charts for Participation in Conformation

PART I is a quick reference of the dogs you've owned over the years. Each entry has a line to note the corresponding page number where the detailed information of each dog can be found. That information will be in Part II of this book. Part I concludes with charts to keep track of hopeful pups, heat cycles, and stud services offered.

PART II provides the details for each dog, from basic information such as their date of birth and registration number, to details about titles and awards earned, health testing, vaccinations given, medications needed, daily routine, and more! There are six pages per dog, and space for 20 dogs.

PART III includes charts to record the details of your dog's participation in the sport of conformation. Heading to a dog show? Stash the book in your grooming bag for quick access to take notes at the show site. You'll want to record the shows you attend, the name of the judge, how your dog placed, and points earned. Each chart follows with a blank page to journal your thoughts about the event and judging. As you enter more shows over the months and years, you'll be happy to look back and consult your notes about a particular judge and recall how your dog did on that day. The conformation charts contain the following information:

date of event, name of the show and judge, class entered, placement received, number of dogs in the class, total entry in the show, points earned, group placement, and BIS.

Part III ends with dog safety tips, information on being a canine ambassador, and a phone/address book.

How to adapt the show charts to other canine sports events:

There are numerous sports events in which your canine companions may participate such as obedience, rally, and agility. To adapt these charts to other events, modify the column headers for your sport and note the name of the organization and event in the space provided at the top of each chart.

SAMPLE show chart is found on page 141.

May this book be a treasured companion as you record the memories and milestones of your beloved dogs!

The Ribbon That Runs Through History

ITS MEANING, PURPOSE, AND GOAL

Who would have thought that holding the winning ribbon could bring a person so much joy! But what exactly does the ribbon symbolize? Why do we seek it, and how does its meaning spur us on to become better exhibitors, competitors, breeders, and dog owners? Let's unravel the ribbon and follow the thread through history, and look behind the scenes of a dog show to better understand what this piece of colorful fabric is really all about.

Have you ever wondered when, where, and why dog shows began? Dennis Homes, the breed historian from the UK Cavalier Club, shares his thoughts:

> There is no single animal species on Earth that is as diverse in both size and appearance as a dog. From the tiny Chihuahua to the Neapolitan Mastiff or the Chinese Crested to the Great Dane, they differ so greatly and yet they are all the same species. Nobody knows for sure how the human/canine bond first came about and for many years experts believed that domestication first occurred around twelve thousand years ago. However, recent archaeological digs in places as far apart as Belgium and Eastern Russia have discovered fossilized remains of domestic dogs in early human encampments that date back to around twenty five thousand years ago. How canine domestication came about is the subject of much speculation but it does appear that dogs evolved from a wolf type ancestor.

> Dogs were probably first used by humans for work functions such as guarding, herding, retrieving, catching vermin, etc. Those that excelled at certain functions were most likely bred with others that had a similar trait and over time this is how certain breed types evolved. It wasn't until around five hundred years ago that dogs were bred purely for their looks, and these were probably only among companion pets of ladies from wealthy or aristocratic families. By and large most dogs were bred for their working abilities.

> Showing dogs, otherwise known as the "sport of conformation", did not start until around the mid 1800s. The earliest known record of a dog show was in 1859 in Newcastle-upon-Tyne in England where Pointers and Setters were exhibited. There soon followed many other small shows where breeders were able to exhibit their dogs and display to other enthusiasts what type of dogs their kennels were producing. Although breeders were competing against each other the primary motive of these early dog shows was to display their dogs to the public at large.

> There was no registration system or keeping of pedigrees at this time, so as these shows started to become more popular the English Kennel Club was set up in 1873 to provide rules and regulations for dog shows and to provide an accurate register of pedigrees. Dog shows were also starting to gain popularity in the United States and in 1884 the American Kennel Club (AKC) was established to maintain breeding records of purebred dogs in the United States. In 1911 the Federation Cynologique Internationle (FCI) was established; it is based in Belgium and oversees the rules of national kennel clubs from around 75 different countries.

> Throughout the twentieth century dog shows gained huge popularity all over the world and to many people it is regarded as a sport. Obviously sport is closely linked with competitiveness, which in turn leads to rivalry. The terms "sportsmanship" and "sportsmanlike" are linked to the word "fairness" as epitomized in the true spirit of the Olympic Games. Competitiveness in this sense encourages people to strive to improve their personal best, to respect one's opponent, and to graciously accept a win or a loss. However, the downside of competitiveness is where rivalry leads to jealousy. If dog showing is to be likened to a sport then it is imperative that there should be friendly rivalry and fairness, as at the end of the day we are dealing with living animals and the welfare of these animals should always be our number one priority. Showing dogs, as shown in the original purpose, should be about exhibitors and breeders striving to improve their dogs in breed type, appearance, soundness and, most importantly, health.

These days, the object of the sport often appears to be simply about winning in the ring. Yet knowing the history behind the ribbons, as Dennis Homes shared, reminds us to see the bigger picture and focus on the original purpose of the sport of conformation: choosing those dogs worthy to carry on bloodlines and the betterment of purebred dogs. That is where true success awaits, and winning ribbons for everyone involved! Whether we're planning a breeding, choosing our next hopeful puppy, organizing a show, or entering the ring with our beloved show dogs, we must allow the original goal to shine through and spur us on to good sportsmanship and excellence in all we do. This same principle would apply to any event such as agility, obedience, or rally. But we cannot achieve this on our own—as the saying goes, "it takes a village"! Dedicated breeders, mentors, exhibitors, judges, and all those who contribute to this wonderful sport have a role to play, and we all need each other to make the show a success. I'm also reminded of the all volunteers and club members who tirelessly work behind the scenes to ensure that the show runs smoothly, and that everyone is safe and having a good time, including our dogs.

The next time we are privileged to participate in a dog show event, let's pause for a moment and recall the rich history behind the ribbon we long to hold. Apart from that, the ribbons are only meaningless pieces of fabric that collect dust, but the memories they make and the meaning they hold is what will last forever. I wish you all glorious success and a rainbow of winning ribbons. But mostly, I wish you to simply enjoy your dogs.

You win or you learn.
—J.J. Clark, Olympic Coach

Staying organized is essential to the multi-dog home, and part of being a responsible dog owner. Strong, detailed note keeping of sire and dam, health testing completed, and litters gives us valuable information which we can consult at a moment's notice. Another important reason to keep records of our dogs and litters is that it is an AKC requirement. This book was designed with that in mind. The following information on this page was prepared by and reprinted with the permission of the American Kennel Club.

Each person or firm who owns, breeds, or sells dogs that are AKC-registrable must keep accurate, up-to-date records of all transactions involving these dogs. There must be no doubt as to the identity of any individual dog or as to the parentage of a particular dog or litter.

The AKC recommends common-sense practices for those who regularly have multiple dogs or litters on their premises, including:

Permanent identification of each dog, with tattoos, microchips, marking, or tagging.

Isolation of bitches in season.

Segregation of litters whelped near the same date.

The AKC requires the owner of an AKC-registered dog to maintain the following information:

Breed

Registered name and number (or litter number if not registered)

Sex, color and markings

Date of birth

Names and numbers of sire and dam

Name of breeder

Name and address of person from whom directly acquired

Date of acquisition

Date and duration of lease, if any

The owner of a dog which is bred must record:

Date and place of mating

Names of persons handling mating

Registered name and number of dog to which mated

Name and address of its owner

The owner of a litter must record:

Date of whelping

Number of puppies whelped by sex and by color and markings

Litter registration number

Date of sale, gift or death of each puppy so described

Name and address of person acquiring each puppy so described

Kinds of papers and date supplied

Registered name and number of each puppy registered by breeder

Our Dogs

Name:_____Dog's History on page _____

Color/Markings: _____ Date Born: _____ Date Deceased: _____

Sire X Dam: _____

Name:_____Dog's History on page _____

Color/Markings: _____ Date Born: _____ Date Deceased: _____

Sire X Dam: _____

Name:_____Dog's History on page _____

Color/Markings: _____ Date Born: _____ Date Deceased: _____

Sire X Dam: _____

Name:_____Dog's History on page _____

Color/Markings: _____ Date Born: _____ Date Deceased: _____

Sire X Dam: _____

Name:_____Dog's History on page _____

Color/Markings: _____ Date Born: _____ Date Deceased: _____

Sire X Dam: _____

Name:_____Dog's History on page _____

Color/Markings: _____ Date Born: _____ Date Deceased: _____

Sire X Dam: _____

Name:_____Dog's History on page _____

Color/Markings: _____ Date Born: _____ Date Deceased: _____

Sire X Dam: _____

Name:_____Dog's History on page _____

Color/Markings: _____ Date Born: _____ Date Deceased: _____

Sire X Dam: _____

Our Dogs

Name:_____Dog's History on page _____

Color/Markings: _____ Date Born: _____ Date Deceased: _____

Sire X Dam: _____

Name:_____Dog's History on page _____

Color/Markings: _____ Date Born: _____ Date Deceased: _____

Sire X Dam: _____

Name:_____Dog's History on page _____

Color/Markings: _____ Date Born: _____ Date Deceased: _____

Sire X Dam: _____

Name:_____Dog's History on page _____

Color/Markings: _____ Date Born: _____ Date Deceased: _____

Sire X Dam: _____

Name:_____Dog's History on page _____

Color/Markings: _____ Date Born: _____ Date Deceased: _____

Sire X Dam: _____

Name:_____Dog's History on page _____

Color/Markings: _____ Date Born: _____ Date Deceased: _____

Sire X Dam: _____

Name:_____Dog's History on page _____

Color/Markings: _____ Date Born: _____ Date Deceased: _____

Sire X Dam: _____

Name:_____Dog's History on page _____

Color/Markings: _____ Date Born: _____ Date Deceased: _____

Sire X Dam: _____

Our Dogs

Name:_____ Dog's History on page _____

Color/Markings: _____ Date Born: _____ Date Deceased: _____

Sire X Dam: _____

Name:_____ Dog's History on page _____

Color/Markings: _____ Date Born: _____ Date Deceased: _____

Sire X Dam: _____

Name:_____ Dog's History on page _____

Color/Markings: _____ Date Born: _____ Date Deceased: _____

Sire X Dam: _____

Name:_____ Dog's History on page _____

Color/Markings: _____ Date Born: _____ Date Deceased: _____

Sire X Dam: _____

Name:_____ Dog's History on page _____

Color/Markings: _____ Date Born: _____ Date Deceased: _____

Sire X Dam: _____

Name:_____ Dog's History on page _____

Color/Markings: _____ Date Born: _____ Date Deceased: _____

Sire X Dam: _____

Name:_____ Dog's History on page _____

Color/Markings: _____ Date Born: _____ Date Deceased: _____

Sire X Dam: _____

Our Hopeful Puppies

Name of Puppy	Date of Birth	Sire X Dam	Date of Transfer, if any	Notes

Our Hopeful Puppies

Name of Puppy	Date of Birth	Sire X Dam	Date of Transfer, if any	Notes

Heat Cycles

Date of Heat	Name of Bitch	Bred to	Dates of Breeding	Missed	# of Puppies	
					Male	Female

Heat Cycles

Date of Heat	Name of Bitch	Bred to	Dates of Breeding	Missed	# of Puppies	
					Male	Female

Heat Cycles

Date of Heat	Name of Bitch	Bred to	Dates of Breeding	Missed	# of Puppies	
					Male	Female

Heat Cycles

Date of Heat	Name of Bitch	Bred to	Dates of Breeding	Missed	# of Puppies	
					Male	Female

Heat Cycles

Date of Heat	Name of Bitch	Bred to	Dates of Breeding	Missed	# of Puppies	
					Male	Female

Heat Cycles

Date of Heat	Name of Bitch	Bred to	Dates of Breeding	Missed	# of Puppies	
					Male	Female

Stud Service

Date	Name of Dog	Bred to	Puppies		Fee
			# of Males	# of Females	

Stud Service

Date	Name of Dog	Bred to	Puppies		Fee
			# of Males	# of Females	

Photo of My Beloved Dog

Registered Name _____ Call Name _____

Dog Information

Name _____ DOB _____

AKC# _____ Other registry # _____

Breed _____ Color/Markings _____

Sex _____ DNA# _____ Microchip# _____

Owner(s) _____

Contact _____

Breeder(s) _____

Contact _____

Date of Acquisition _____ Date & Duration of Lease, if any _____

Sire x Dam _____

Health, Nutrition, Routine

Medications: _____

Heartworm Medication: _____

Flea/Tick Prevention: _____

Allergies: _____

Food Brand & Type (wet and/or dry; raw and/or cooked; homemade or commercial): _____

_____

Supplements & Treats _____

Feeding Schedule: _____

Routine/Likes/Dislikes: _____

_____

Medical Insurance Policy: _____

EMERGENCY CONTACT: _____

Achievements, Memories, and Milestones

Record you dog's Champion titles, Awards and Honors, Best In Show, Certifications, training classes completed, or any achievements, memories, and milestones.

Achievement: _____ Date earned: _____

Achievement: _____ Date earned: _____

Achievement: _____ Date earned: _____

Achievement: _____ Date earned: _____

Achievement: _____ Date earned: _____

Achievement: _____ Date earned: _____

Achievement: _____ Date earned: _____

Achievement: _____ Date earned: _____

Achievement: _____ Date earned: _____

Achievement: _____ Date earned: _____

Achievement: _____ Date earned: _____

Achievement: _____ Date earned: _____

Notes _____

_____

_____

_____

_____

_____

_____

Vaccination Record

Name _____

Age										
Date										
Distemper										
Adenovirus										
Parainfluenza										
Parvovirus										
Coronavirus										
Leptospirosis										
Bordetella										
Lyme Disease										
Rabies										
Antibody titer tests (state which tests are run)										

Notes _____

_____

_____

_____

_____

_____

Health Testing/Health History

Name _____

Date	Weight	Name of Test/Reason for Visit	Results	Veterinarian

Health Testing/Health History

Name _____

Date	Weight	Name of Test/Reason for Visit	Results	Veterinarian

Photo of My Beloved Dog

Registered Name _____ Call Name _____

Dog Information

Name _____ DOB _____

AKC# _____ Other registry # _____

Breed _____ Color/Markings _____

Sex_____DNA#_____Microchip#_____

Owner(s) _____

Contact _____

Breeder(s) _____

Contact _____

Date of Acquisition _____ Date & Duration of Lease, if any _____

Sire x Dam _____

Health, Nutrition, Routine

Medications: _____

Heartworm Medication: _____

Flea/Tick Prevention: _____

Allergies: _____

Food Brand & Type (wet and/or dry; raw and/or cooked; homemade or commercial): _____

_____

Supplements & Treats _____

Feeding Schedule: _____

Routine/Likes/Dislikes: _____

_____

Medical Insurance Policy: _____

EMERGENCY CONTACT: _____

Achievements, Memories, and Milestones

Record you dog's Champion titles, Awards and Honors, Best In Show, Certifications, training classes completed, or any achievements, memories, and milestones.

Achievement: _____ Date earned: _____

Achievement: _____ Date earned: _____

Achievement: _____ Date earned: _____

Achievement: _____ Date earned: _____

Achievement: _____ Date earned: _____

Achievement: _____ Date earned: _____

Achievement: _____ Date earned: _____

Achievement: _____ Date earned: _____

Achievement: _____ Date earned: _____

Achievement: _____ Date earned: _____

Achievement: _____ Date earned: _____

Achievement: _____ Date earned: _____

Notes _____

_____

_____

_____

_____

_____

Vaccination Record

Name _____

Age											
Date											
Distemper											
Adenovirus											
Parainfluenza											
Parvovirus											
Coronavirus											
Leptospirosis											
Bordetella											
Lyme Disease											
Rabies											
Antibody titer tests (state which tests are run)											

Notes _____

_____

_____

_____

_____

_____

Health Testing/Health History

Name _____

Date	Weight	Name of Test/Reason for Visit	Results	Veterinarian

Health Testing/Health History

Name _____

Date	Weight	Name of Test/Reason for Visit	Results	Veterinarian

Photo of My Beloved Dog

Registered Name _____ Call Name _____

Dog Information

Name _____ DOB _____

AKC# _____ Other registry # _____

Breed _____ Color/Markings _____

Sex_____DNA#_____Microchip#_____

Owner(s) _____

Contact _____

Breeder(s) _____

Contact _____

Date of Acquisition _____ Date & Duration of Lease, if any _____

Sire x Dam _____

Health, Nutrition, Routine

Medications: _____

Heartworm Medication: _____

Flea/Tick Prevention: _____

Allergies: _____

Food Brand & Type (wet and/or dry; raw and/or cooked; homemade or commercial): _____

_____

Supplements & Treats _____

Feeding Schedule: _____

Routine/Likes/Dislikes: _____

_____

Medical Insurance Policy: _____

EMERGENCY CONTACT: _____

Achievements, Memories, and Milestones

Record you dog's Champion titles, Awards and Honors, Best In Show, Certifications, training classes completed, or any achievements, memories, and milestones.

Achievement: _____ Date earned: _____

Achievement: _____ Date earned: _____

Achievement: _____ Date earned: _____

Achievement: _____ Date earned: _____

Achievement: _____ Date earned: _____

Achievement: _____ Date earned: _____

Achievement: _____ Date earned: _____

Achievement: _____ Date earned: _____

Achievement: _____ Date earned: _____

Achievement: _____ Date earned: _____

Achievement: _____ Date earned: _____

Achievement: _____ Date earned: _____

Notes _____

_____

_____

_____

_____

_____

Vaccination Record

Name _____

Age										
Date										
Distemper										
Adenovirus										
Parainfluenza										
Parvovirus										
Coronavirus										
Leptospirosis										
Bordetella										
Lyme Disease										
Rabies										
Antibody titer tests (state which tests are run)										

Notes _____

_____

_____

_____

_____

Health Testing/Health History

Name _____

Date	Weight	Name of Test/Reason for Visit	Results	Veterinarian

Health Testing/Health History

Name _____

Date	Weight	Name of Test/Reason for Visit	Results	Veterinarian

Photo of My Beloved Dog

Registered Name _____ Call Name _____

Dog Information

Name _____ DOB _____

AKC# _____ Other registry # _____

Breed _____ Color/Markings _____

Sex_____DNA#_____Microchip#_____

Owner(s) _____

Contact _____

Breeder(s) _____

Contact _____

Date of Acquisition _____ Date & Duration of Lease, if any _____

Sire x Dam _____

Health, Nutrition, Routine

Medications: _____

Heartworm Medication: _____

Flea/Tick Prevention: _____

Allergies: _____

Food Brand & Type (wet and/or dry; raw and/or cooked; homemade or commercial): _____

_____

Supplements & Treats _____

Feeding Schedule: _____

Routine/Likes/Dislikes: _____

_____

Medical Insurance Policy: _____

EMERGENCY CONTACT: _____

40

Achievements, Memories, and Milestones

Record you dog's Champion titles, Awards and Honors, Best In Show, Certifications, training classes completed, or any achievements, memories, and milestones.

Achievement: _____ Date earned: _____

Achievement: _____ Date earned: _____

Achievement: _____ Date earned: _____

Achievement: _____ Date earned: _____

Achievement: _____ Date earned: _____

Achievement: _____ Date earned: _____

Achievement: _____ Date earned: _____

Achievement: _____ Date earned: _____

Achievement: _____ Date earned: _____

Achievement: _____ Date earned: _____

Achievement: _____ Date earned: _____

Achievement: _____ Date earned: _____

Notes _____

_____

_____

_____

_____

_____

_____

Vaccination Record

Name _____

Age										
Date										
Distemper										
Adenovirus										
Parainfluenza										
Parvovirus										
Coronavirus										
Leptospirosis										
Bordetella										
Lyme Disease										
Rabies										
Antibody titer tests (state which tests are run)										

Notes _____

_____

_____

_____

_____

Health Testing/Health History

Name _____

Date	Weight	Name of Test/Reason for Visit	Results	Veterinarian

Health Testing/Health History

Name _____

Date	Weight	Name of Test/Reason for Visit	Results	Veterinarian

Photo of My Beloved Dog

Registered Name _____ Call Name _____

Dog Information

Name _____ DOB _____

AKC# _____ Other registry # _____

Breed _____ Color/Markings _____

Sex_____DNA#_____Microchip#_____

Owner(s) _____

Contact _____

Breeder(s) _____

Contact _____

Date of Acquisition _____ Date & Duration of Lease, if any _____

Sire x Dam _____

Health, Nutrition, Routine

Medications: _____

Heartworm Medication: _____

Flea/Tick Prevention: _____

Allergies: _____

Food Brand & Type (wet and/or dry; raw and/or cooked; homemade or commercial): _____

_____

Supplements & Treats _____

Feeding Schedule: _____

Routine/Likes/Dislikes: _____

_____

Medical Insurance Policy: _____

EMERGENCY CONTACT: _____

Achievements, Memories, and Milestones

Record you dog's Champion titles, Awards and Honors, Best In Show, Certifications, training classes completed, or any achievements, memories, and milestones.

Achievement: _____ Date earned: _____

Achievement: _____ Date earned: _____

Achievement: _____ Date earned: _____

Achievement: _____ Date earned: _____

Achievement: _____ Date earned: _____

Achievement: _____ Date earned: _____

Achievement: _____ Date earned: _____

Achievement: _____ Date earned: _____

Achievement: _____ Date earned: _____

Achievement: _____ Date earned: _____

Achievement: _____ Date earned: _____

Achievement: _____ Date earned: _____

Notes _____

_____

_____

_____

_____

_____

Vaccination Record

Name _____

Age									
Date									
Distemper									
Adenovirus									
Parainfluenza									
Parvovirus									
Coronavirus									
Leptospirosis									
Bordetella									
Lyme Disease									
Rabies									
Antibody titer tests (state which tests are run)									

Notes _____

_____

_____

_____

_____

_____

48

Health Testing/Health History

Name _____

Date	Weight	Name of Test/Reason for Visit	Results	Veterinarian

Health Testing/Health History

Name _____

Date	Weight	Name of Test/Reason for Visit	Results	Veterinarian

Photo of My Beloved Dog

Registered Name _____ Call Name _____

Dog Information

Name _____ DOB _____

AKC# _____ Other registry # _____

Breed _____ Color/Markings _____

Sex_____DNA#_____Microchip#_____

Owner(s) _____

Contact _____

Breeder(s) _____

Contact _____

Date of Acquisition _____ Date & Duration of Lease, if any _____

Sire x Dam _____

Health, Nutrition, Routine

Medications: _____

Heartworm Medication: _____

Flea/Tick Prevention: _____

Allergies: _____

Food Brand & Type (wet and/or dry; raw and/or cooked; homemade or commercial): _____

_____

Supplements & Treats _____

Feeding Schedule: _____

Routine/Likes/Dislikes: _____

_____

Medical Insurance Policy: _____

EMERGENCY CONTACT: _____

Achievements, Memories, and Milestones

Record you dog's Champion titles, Awards and Honors, Best In Show, Certifications, training classes completed, or any achievements, memories, and milestones.

Achievement: _____ Date earned: _____

Achievement: _____ Date earned: _____

Achievement: _____ Date earned: _____

Achievement: _____ Date earned: _____

Achievement: _____ Date earned: _____

Achievement: _____ Date earned: _____

Achievement: _____ Date earned: _____

Achievement: _____ Date earned: _____

Achievement: _____ Date earned: _____

Achievement: _____ Date earned: _____

Achievement: _____ Date earned: _____

Achievement: _____ Date earned: _____

Notes _____

_____

_____

_____

_____

_____

Vaccination Record

Name _____

Age										
Date										
Distemper										
Adenovirus										
Parainfluenza										
Parvovirus										
Coronavirus										
Leptospirosis										
Bordetella										
Lyme Disease										
Rabies										
Antibody titer tests (state which tests are run)										

Notes _____
_____
_____
_____
_____
_____

Health Testing/Health History

Name _____

Date	Weight	Name of Test/Reason for Visit	Results	Veterinarian

55

Health Testing/Health History

Name _____

Date	Weight	Name of Test/Reason for Visit	Results	Veterinarian

Photo of My Beloved Dog

Registered Name _____ Call Name _____

Dog Information

Name _____ DOB _____

AKC# _____ Other registry # _____

Breed _____ Color/Markings _____

Sex_____DNA#_____Microchip#_____

Owner(s) _____

Contact _____

Breeder(s) _____

Contact _____

Date of Acquisition _____ Date & Duration of Lease, if any _____

Sire x Dam _____

Health, Nutrition, Routine

Medications: _____

Heartworm Medication: _____

Flea/Tick Prevention: _____

Allergies: _____

Food Brand & Type (wet and/or dry; raw and/or cooked; homemade or commercial): _____

_____

Supplements & Treats _____

Feeding Schedule: _____

Routine/Likes/Dislikes: _____

_____

Medical Insurance Policy: _____

EMERGENCY CONTACT: _____

58

Achievements, Memories, and Milestones

Record you dog's Champion titles, Awards and Honors, Best In Show, Certifications, training classes completed, or any achievements, memories, and milestones.

Achievement: _____ Date earned: _____

Achievement: _____ Date earned: _____

Achievement: _____ Date earned: _____

Achievement: _____ Date earned: _____

Achievement: _____ Date earned: _____

Achievement: _____ Date earned: _____

Achievement: _____ Date earned: _____

Achievement: _____ Date earned: _____

Achievement: _____ Date earned: _____

Achievement: _____ Date earned: _____

Achievement: _____ Date earned: _____

Achievement: _____ Date earned: _____

Notes _____

_____

_____

_____

_____

_____

Vaccination Record

Name _____

Age									
Date									
Distemper									
Adenovirus									
Parainfluenza									
Parvovirus									
Coronavirus									
Leptospirosis									
Bordetella									
Lyme Disease									
Rabies									
Antibody titer tests (state which tests are run)									

Notes _____

_____

_____

_____

_____

Health Testing/Health History

Name _____

Date	Weight	Name of Test/Reason for Visit	Results	Veterinarian

Health Testing/Health History

Name _____

Date	Weight	Name of Test/Reason for Visit	Results	Veterinarian

Health Testing/Health History

Name _____

Photo of My Beloved Dog

Registered Name _____ Call Name _____

Dog Information

Name _____ DOB _____

AKC# _____ Other registry # _____

Breed _____ Color/Markings _____

Sex_____DNA#_____Microchip#_____

Owner(s) _____

Contact _____

Breeder(s) _____

Contact _____

Date of Acquisition _____ Date & Duration of Lease, if any _____

Sire x Dam _____

Health, Nutrition, Routine

Medications: _____

Heartworm Medication: _____

Flea/Tick Prevention: _____

Allergies: _____

Food Brand & Type (wet and/or dry; raw and/or cooked; homemade or commercial): _____

_____

Supplements & Treats _____

Feeding Schedule: _____

Routine/Likes/Dislikes: _____

_____

Medical Insurance Policy: _____

EMERGENCY CONTACT: _____

64

Achievements, Memories, and Milestones

Record you dog's Champion titles, Awards and Honors, Best In Show, Certifications, training classes completed, or any achievements, memories, and milestones.

Achievement: _____ Date earned: _____

Achievement: _____ Date earned: _____

Achievement: _____ Date earned: _____

Achievement: _____ Date earned: _____

Achievement: _____ Date earned: _____

Achievement: _____ Date earned: _____

Achievement: _____ Date earned: _____

Achievement: _____ Date earned: _____

Achievement: _____ Date earned: _____

Achievement: _____ Date earned: _____

Achievement: _____ Date earned: _____

Achievement: _____ Date earned: _____

Notes _____

_____

_____

_____

_____

_____

Vaccination Record

Name _____

Age										
Date										
Distemper										
Adenovirus										
Parainfluenza										
Parvovirus										
Coronavirus										
Leptospirosis										
Bordetella										
Lyme Disease										
Rabies										
Antibody titer tests (state which tests are run)										

Notes _____

_____

_____

_____

_____

_____

Health Testing/Health History

Name _____

Date	Weight	Name of Test/Reason for Visit	Results	Veterinarian

Health Testing/Health History

Name _____

Date	Weight	Name of Test/Reason for Visit	Results	Veterinarian

Photo of My Beloved Dog

Registered Name _____ Call Name _____

Dog Information

Name _____ DOB _____

AKC# _____ Other registry # _____

Breed _____ Color/Markings _____

Sex_____DNA#_____Microchip#_____

Owner(s) _____

Contact _____

Breeder(s) _____

Contact _____

Date of Acquisition _____ Date & Duration of Lease, if any _____

Sire x Dam _____

Health, Nutrition, Routine

Medications: _____

Heartworm Medication: _____

Flea/Tick Prevention: _____

Allergies: _____

Food Brand & Type (wet and/or dry; raw and/or cooked; homemade or commercial): _____

_____

Supplements & Treats _____

Feeding Schedule: _____

Routine/Likes/Dislikes: _____

_____

Medical Insurance Policy: _____

EMERGENCY CONTACT: _____

Achievements, Memories, and Milestones

Record you dog's Champion titles, Awards and Honors, Best In Show, Certifications, training classes completed, or any achievements, memories, and milestones.

Achievement: _____ Date earned: _____

Achievement: _____ Date earned: _____

Achievement: _____ Date earned: _____

Achievement: _____ Date earned: _____

Achievement: _____ Date earned: _____

Achievement: _____ Date earned: _____

Achievement: _____ Date earned: _____

Achievement: _____ Date earned: _____

Achievement: _____ Date earned: _____

Achievement: _____ Date earned: _____

Achievement: _____ Date earned: _____

Achievement: _____ Date earned: _____

Notes _____

_____

_____

_____

_____

_____

Vaccination Record

Name _____

Age									
Date									
Distemper									
Adenovirus									
Parainfluenza									
Parvovirus									
Coronavirus									
Leptospirosis									
Bordetella									
Lyme Disease									
Rabies									
Antibody titer tests (state which tests are run)									

Notes _____

_____

_____

_____

_____

72

Health Testing/Health History

Name _____

Date	Weight	Name of Test/Reason for Visit	Results	Veterinarian

Health Testing/Health History

Name _____

Date	Weight	Name of Test/Reason for Visit	Results	Veterinarian

Photo of My Beloved Dog

Registered Name _____ Call Name _____

Dog Information

Name _____ DOB _____

AKC# _____ Other registry # _____

Breed _____ Color/Markings _____

Sex_____DNA#_____Microchip#_____

Owner(s) _____

Contact _____

Breeder(s) _____

Contact _____

Date of Acquisition _____ Date & Duration of Lease, if any _____

Sire x Dam _____

Health, Nutrition, Routine

Medications: _____

Heartworm Medication: _____

Flea/Tick Prevention: _____

Allergies: _____

Food Brand & Type (wet and/or dry; raw and/or cooked; homemade or commercial): _____

_____

Supplements & Treats _____

Feeding Schedule: _____

Routine/Likes/Dislikes: _____

_____

Medical Insurance Policy: _____

EMERGENCY CONTACT: _____

76

Achievements, Memories, and Milestones

Record you dog's Champion titles, Awards and Honors, Best In Show, Certifications, training classes completed, or any achievements, memories, and milestones.

Achievement: _____ Date earned: _____

Achievement: _____ Date earned: _____

Achievement: _____ Date earned: _____

Achievement: _____ Date earned: _____

Achievement: _____ Date earned: _____

Achievement: _____ Date earned: _____

Achievement: _____ Date earned: _____

Achievement: _____ Date earned: _____

Achievement: _____ Date earned: _____

Achievement: _____ Date earned: _____

Achievement: _____ Date earned: _____

Achievement: _____ Date earned: _____

Notes _____

_____

_____

_____

_____

_____

Vaccination Record

Name _____

Age										
Date										
Distemper										
Adenovirus										
Parainfluenza										
Parvovirus										
Coronavirus										
Leptospirosis										
Bordetella										
Lyme Disease										
Rabies										
Antibody titer tests (state which tests are run)										

Notes _____

_____

_____

_____

_____

Health Testing/Health History

Name _____

Date	Weight	Name of Test/Reason for Visit	Results	Veterinarian

Health Testing/Health History

Name _____

Date	Weight	Name of Test/Reason for Visit	Results	Veterinarian

Photo of My Beloved Dog

Registered Name _____ Call Name _____

Dog Information

Name _____ DOB _____

AKC# _____ Other registry # _____

Breed _____ Color/Markings _____

Sex _____ DNA# _____ Microchip# _____

Owner(s) _____

Contact _____

Breeder(s) _____

Contact _____

Date of Acquisition _____ Date & Duration of Lease, if any _____

Sire x Dam _____

Health, Nutrition, Routine

Medications: _____

Heartworm Medication: _____

Flea/Tick Prevention: _____

Allergies: _____

Food Brand & Type (wet and/or dry; raw and/or cooked; homemade or commercial): _____

_____

Supplements & Treats _____

Feeding Schedule: _____

Routine/Likes/Dislikes: _____

_____

Medical Insurance Policy: _____

EMERGENCY CONTACT: _____

Achievements, Memories, and Milestones

Record you dog's Champion titles, Awards and Honors, Best In Show, Certifications, training classes completed, or any achievements, memories, and milestones.

Achievement: _____ Date earned: _____

Achievement: _____ Date earned: _____

Achievement: _____ Date earned: _____

Achievement: _____ Date earned: _____

Achievement: _____ Date earned: _____

Achievement: _____ Date earned: _____

Achievement: _____ Date earned: _____

Achievement: _____ Date earned: _____

Achievement: _____ Date earned: _____

Achievement: _____ Date earned: _____

Achievement: _____ Date earned: _____

Achievement: _____ Date earned: _____

Notes _____

_____

_____

_____

_____

_____

Vaccination Record

Name _____

Age									
Date									
Distemper									
Adenovirus									
Parainfluenza									
Parvovirus									
Coronavirus									
Leptospirosis									
Bordetella									
Lyme Disease									
Rabies									
Antibody titer tests (state which tests are run)									

Notes _____

_____

_____

_____

_____

_____

Health Testing/Health History

Name _____

Date	Weight	Name of Test/Reason for Visit	Results	Veterinarian

Health Testing/Health History

Name _____

Date	Weight	Name of Test/Reason for Visit	Results	Veterinarian

86

Photo of My Beloved Dog

Registered Name _____ Call Name _____

Dog Information

Name _____ DOB _____

AKC# _____ Other registry # _____

Breed _____ Color/Markings _____

Sex_____DNA#_____Microchip#_____

Owner(s) _____

Contact _____

Breeder(s) _____

Contact _____

Date of Acquisition _____ Date & Duration of Lease, if any _____

Sire x Dam _____

Health, Nutrition, Routine

Medications: _____

Heartworm Medication: _____

Flea/Tick Prevention: _____

Allergies: _____

Food Brand & Type (wet and/or dry; raw and/or cooked; homemade or commercial): _____

_____

Supplements & Treats _____

Feeding Schedule: _____

Routine/Likes/Dislikes: _____

_____

Medical Insurance Policy: _____

EMERGENCY CONTACT: _____

Achievements, Memories, and Milestones

Record you dog's Champion titles, Awards and Honors, Best In Show, Certifications, training classes completed, or any achievements, memories, and milestones.

Achievement: _____ Date earned: _____

Achievement: _____ Date earned: _____

Achievement: _____ Date earned: _____

Achievement: _____ Date earned: _____

Achievement: _____ Date earned: _____

Achievement: _____ Date earned: _____

Achievement: _____ Date earned: _____

Achievement: _____ Date earned: _____

Achievement: _____ Date earned: _____

Achievement: _____ Date earned: _____

Achievement: _____ Date earned: _____

Achievement: _____ Date earned: _____

Notes _____

_____

_____

_____

_____

_____

Vaccination Record

Name _____

Age										
Date										
Distemper										
Adenovirus										
Parainfluenza										
Parvovirus										
Coronavirus										
Leptospirosis										
Bordetella										
Lyme Disease										
Rabies										
Antibody titer tests (state which tests are run)										

Notes _____

_____

_____

_____

_____

_____

Health Testing/Health History

Name _____

Date	Weight	Name of Test/Reason for Visit	Results	Veterinarian

Health Testing/Health History

Name _____

Date	Weight	Name of Test/Reason for Visit	Results	Veterinarian

Photo of My Beloved Dog

Registered Name _____ Call Name _____

Dog Information

Name _____ DOB _____

AKC# _____ Other registry # _____

Breed _____ Color/Markings _____

Sex_____DNA#_____Microchip#_____

Owner(s) _____

Contact _____

Breeder(s) _____

Contact _____

Date of Acquisition _____ Date & Duration of Lease, if any _____

Sire x Dam _____

Health, Nutrition, Routine

Medications: _____

Heartworm Medication: _____

Flea/Tick Prevention: _____

Allergies: _____

Food Brand & Type (wet and/or dry; raw and/or cooked; homemade or commercial): _____

_____

Supplements & Treats _____

Feeding Schedule: _____

Routine/Likes/Dislikes: _____

_____

Medical Insurance Policy: _____

EMERGENCY CONTACT: _____

Achievements, Memories, and Milestones

Record you dog's Champion titles, Awards and Honors, Best In Show, Certifications, training classes completed, or any achievements, memories, and milestones.

Achievement: _____ Date earned: _____

Achievement: _____ Date earned: _____

Achievement: _____ Date earned: _____

Achievement: _____ Date earned: _____

Achievement: _____ Date earned: _____

Achievement: _____ Date earned: _____

Achievement: _____ Date earned: _____ _____

Achievement: _____ Date earned: _____

Achievement: _____ Date earned: _____

Achievement: _____ Date earned: _____

Achievement: _____ Date earned: _____

Achievement: _____ Date earned: _____

Notes _____

_____

_____

_____

_____

_____

Vaccination Record

Name _____

Age									
Date									
Distemper									
Adenovirus									
Parainfluenza									
Parvovirus									
Coronavirus									
Leptospirosis									
Bordetella									
Lyme Disease									
Rabies									
Antibody titer tests (state which tests are run)									

Notes _____

_____

_____

_____

_____

Health Testing/Health History

Name _____

Date	Weight	Name of Test/Reason for Visit	Results	Veterinarian

Health Testing/Health History

Name _____

Date	Weight	Name of Test/Reason for Visit	Results	Veterinarian

Photo of My Beloved Dog

Registered Name _____ Call Name _____

Dog Information

Name _____ DOB _____

AKC# _____ Other registry # _____

Breed _____ Color/Markings _____

Sex_____DNA#_____Microchip#_____

Owner(s) _____

Contact _____

Breeder(s) _____

Contact _____

Date of Acquisition _____ Date & Duration of Lease, if any _____

Sire x Dam _____

Health, Nutrition, Routine

Medications: _____

Heartworm Medication: _____

Flea/Tick Prevention: _____

Allergies: _____

Food Brand & Type (wet and/or dry; raw and/or cooked; homemade or commercial): _____

_____

Supplements & Treats _____

Feeding Schedule: _____

Routine/Likes/Dislikes: _____

_____

Medical Insurance Policy: _____

EMERGENCY CONTACT: _____

Achievements, Memories, and Milestones

Record you dog's Champion titles, Awards and Honors, Best In Show, Certifications, training classes completed, or any achievements, memories, and milestones.

Achievement: _____ Date earned: _____

Achievement: _____ Date earned: _____

Achievement: _____ Date earned: _____

Achievement: _____ Date earned: _____

Achievement: _____ Date earned: _____

Achievement: _____ Date earned: _____

Achievement: _____ Date earned: _____

Achievement: _____ Date earned: _____

Achievement: _____ Date earned: _____

Achievement: _____ Date earned: _____

Achievement: _____ Date earned: _____

Achievement: _____ Date earned: _____

Notes _____

_____

_____

_____

_____

_____

Vaccination Record

Name _____

Age									
Date									
Distemper									
Adenovirus									
Parainfluenza									
Parvovirus									
Coronavirus									
Leptospirosis									
Bordetella									
Lyme Disease									
Rabies									
Antibody titer tests (state which tests are run)									

Notes _____

_____

_____

_____

_____

_____

Health Testing/Health History

Name _____

Date	Weight	Name of Test/Reason for Visit	Results	Veterinarian

Health Testing/Health History

Name _____

Date	Weight	Name of Test/Reason for Visit	Results	Veterinarian

Photo of My Beloved Dog

Registered Name _____ Call Name _____

Dog Information

Name _____ DOB _____

AKC# _____ Other registry # _____

Breed _____ Color/Markings _____

Sex_____DNA#_____Microchip#_____

Owner(s) _____

Contact _____

Breeder(s) _____

Contact _____

Date of Acquisition _____ Date & Duration of Lease, if any _____

Sire x Dam _____

Health, Nutrition, Routine

Medications: _____

Heartworm Medication: _____

Flea/Tick Prevention: _____

Allergies: _____

Food Brand & Type (wet and/or dry; raw and/or cooked; homemade or commercial): _____

_____

Supplements & Treats _____

Feeding Schedule: _____

Routine/Likes/Dislikes: _____

_____

Medical Insurance Policy: _____

EMERGENCY CONTACT: _____

Achievements, Memories, and Milestones

Record you dog's Champion titles, Awards and Honors, Best In Show, Certifications, training classes completed, or any achievements, memories, and milestones.

Achievement: _____ Date earned: _____

Achievement: _____ Date earned: _____

Achievement: _____ Date earned: _____

Achievement: _____ Date earned: _____

Achievement: _____ Date earned: _____

Achievement: _____ Date earned: _____

Achievement: _____ Date earned: _____

Achievement: _____ Date earned: _____

Achievement: _____ Date earned: _____

Achievement: _____ Date earned: _____

Achievement: _____ Date earned: _____

Achievement: _____ Date earned: _____

Notes _____

_____

_____

_____

_____

_____

Vaccination Record

Name _____

Age									
Date									
Distemper									
Adenovirus									
Parainfluenza									
Parvovirus									
Coronavirus									
Leptospirosis									
Bordetella									
Lyme Disease									
Rabies									
Antibody titer tests (state which tests are run)									

Notes _____

_____

_____

_____

_____

_____

108

Health Testing/Health History

Name _____

Date	Weight	Name of Test/Reason for Visit	Results	Veterinarian

Health Testing/Health History

Name _____

Date	Weight	Name of Test/Reason for Visit	Results	Veterinarian

Photo of My Beloved Dog

Registered Name _____ Call Name _____

Dog Information

Name _____ DOB _____

AKC# _____ Other registry # _____

Breed _____ Color/Markings _____

Sex_____DNA#_____Microchip#_____

Owner(s) _____

Contact _____

Breeder(s) _____

Contact _____

Date of Acquisition _____ Date & Duration of Lease, if any _____

Sire x Dam _____

Health, Nutrition, Routine

Medications: _____

Heartworm Medication: _____

Flea/Tick Prevention: _____

Allergies: _____

Food Brand & Type (wet and/or dry; raw and/or cooked; homemade or commercial): _____

_____

Supplements & Treats _____

Feeding Schedule: _____

Routine/Likes/Dislikes: _____

_____

Medical Insurance Policy: _____

EMERGENCY CONTACT: _____

Achievements, Memories, and Milestones

Record you dog's Champion titles, Awards and Honors, Best In Show, Certifications, training classes completed, or any achievements, memories, and milestones.

Achievement: _____ Date earned: _____

Achievement: _____ Date earned: _____

Achievement: _____ Date earned: _____

Achievement: _____ Date earned: _____

Achievement: _____ Date earned: _____

Achievement: _____ Date earned: _____

Achievement: _____ Date earned: _____

Achievement: _____ Date earned: _____

Achievement: _____ Date earned: _____

Achievement: _____ Date earned: _____

Achievement: _____ Date earned: _____

Achievement: _____ Date earned: _____

Notes _____

_____

_____

_____

_____

_____

Vaccination Record

Name _____

Age									
Date									
Distemper									
Adenovirus									
Parainfluenza									
Parvovirus									
Coronavirus									
Leptospirosis									
Bordetella									
Lyme Disease									
Rabies									
Antibody titer tests (state which tests are run)									

Notes _____

_____

_____

_____

_____

_____

114

Health Testing/Health History

Name _____

Date	Weight	Name of Test/Reason for Visit	Results	Veterinarian

Health Testing/Health History

Name _____

Date	Weight	Name of Test/Reason for Visit	Results	Veterinarian

Photo of My Beloved Dog

Registered Name _____ Call Name _____

Dog Information

Name _____ DOB _____

AKC# _____ Other registry # _____

Breed _____ Color/Markings _____

Sex_____DNA#_____Microchip#_____

Owner(s) _____

Contact _____

Breeder(s) _____

Contact _____

Date of Acquisition _____ Date & Duration of Lease, if any _____

Sire x Dam _____

Health, Nutrition, Routine

Medications: _____

Heartworm Medication: _____

Flea/Tick Prevention: _____

Allergies: _____

Food Brand & Type (wet and/or dry; raw and/or cooked; homemade or commercial): _____

_____

Supplements & Treats _____

Feeding Schedule: _____

Routine/Likes/Dislikes: _____

_____

Medical Insurance Policy: _____

EMERGENCY CONTACT: _____

Achievements, Memories, and Milestones

Record you dog's Champion titles, Awards and Honors, Best In Show, Certifications, training classes completed, or any achievements, memories, and milestones.

Achievement: _____ Date earned: _____

Achievement: _____ Date earned: _____

Achievement: _____ Date earned: _____

Achievement: _____ Date earned: _____

Achievement: _____ Date earned: _____

Achievement: _____ Date earned: _____

Achievement: _____ Date earned: _____

Achievement: _____ Date earned: _____

Achievement: _____ Date earned: _____

Achievement: _____ Date earned: _____

Achievement: _____ Date earned: _____

Achievement: _____ Date earned: _____

Notes _____

_____

_____

_____

_____

_____

_____

Vaccination Record

Name _____

Age										
Date										
Distemper										
Adenovirus										
Parainfluenza										
Parvovirus										
Coronavirus										
Leptospirosis										
Bordetella										
Lyme Disease										
Rabies										
Antibody titer tests (state which tests are run)										

Notes _____

_____

_____

_____

_____

_____

Health Testing/Health History

Name _____

Date	Weight	Name of Test/Reason for Visit	Results	Veterinarian

Health Testing/Health History

Name _____

Date	Weight	Name of Test/Reason for Visit	Results	Veterinarian

Photo of My Beloved Dog

Registered Name _____ Call Name _____

Dog Information

Name _____ DOB _____

AKC# _____ Other registry # _____

Breed _____ Color/Markings _____

Sex_____DNA#_____Microchip#_____

Owner(s) _____

Contact _____

Breeder(s) _____

Contact _____

Date of Acquisition _____ Date & Duration of Lease, if any _____

Sire x Dam _____

Health, Nutrition, Routine

Medications: _____

Heartworm Medication: _____

Flea/Tick Prevention: _____

Allergies: _____

Food Brand & Type (wet and/or dry; raw and/or cooked; homemade or commercial): _____

_____

Supplements & Treats _____

Feeding Schedule: _____

Routine/Likes/Dislikes: _____

_____

Medical Insurance Policy: _____

EMERGENCY CONTACT: _____

124

Achievements, Memories, and Milestones

Record you dog's Champion titles, Awards and Honors, Best In Show, Certifications, training classes completed, or any achievements, memories, and milestones.

Achievement: _____ Date earned: _____

Achievement: _____ Date earned: _____

Achievement: _____ Date earned: _____

Achievement: _____ Date earned: _____

Achievement: _____ Date earned: _____

Achievement: _____ Date earned: _____

Achievement: _____ Date earned: _____

Achievement: _____ Date earned: _____

Achievement: _____ Date earned: _____

Achievement: _____ Date earned: _____

Achievement: _____ Date earned: _____

Achievement: _____ Date earned: _____

Notes _____

_____

_____

_____

_____

_____

Vaccination Record

Name _____

Age										
Date										
Distemper										
Adenovirus										
Parainfluenza										
Parvovirus										
Coronavirus										
Leptospirosis										
Bordetella										
Lyme Disease										
Rabies										
Antibody titer tests (state which tests are run)										

Notes _____

_____

_____

_____

_____

Health Testing/Health History

Name _____

Date	Weight	Name of Test/Reason for Visit	Results	Veterinarian

Health Testing/Health History

Name _____

Date	Weight	Name of Test/Reason for Visit	Results	Veterinarian

Photo of My Beloved Dog

Registered Name _____ Call Name _____

Dog Information

Name _____ DOB _____

AKC# _____ Other registry # _____

Breed _____ Color/Markings _____

Sex_____DNA#_____Microchip#_____

Owner(s) _____

Contact _____

Breeder(s) _____

Contact _____

Date of Acquisition _____ Date & Duration of Lease, if any _____

Sire x Dam _____

Health, Nutrition, Routine

Medications: _____

Heartworm Medication: _____

Flea/Tick Prevention: _____

Allergies: _____

Food Brand & Type (wet and/or dry; raw and/or cooked; homemade or commercial): _____

_____

Supplements & Treats _____

Feeding Schedule: _____

Routine/Likes/Dislikes: _____

_____

Medical Insurance Policy: _____

EMERGENCY CONTACT: _____

Achievements, Memories, and Milestones

Record you dog's Champion titles, Awards and Honors, Best In Show, Certifications, training classes completed, or any achievements, memories, and milestones.

Achievement: _____ Date earned: _____

Achievement: _____ Date earned: _____

Achievement: _____ Date earned: _____

Achievement: _____ Date earned: _____

Achievement: _____ Date earned: _____

Achievement: _____ Date earned: _____

Achievement: _____ Date earned: _____

Achievement: _____ Date earned: _____

Achievement: _____ Date earned: _____

Achievement: _____ Date earned: _____

Achievement: _____ Date earned: _____

Achievement: _____ Date earned: _____

Notes _____

_____

_____

_____

_____

_____

Vaccination Record

Name _____

Age										
Date										
Distemper										
Adenovirus										
Parainfluenza										
Parvovirus										
Coronavirus										
Leptospirosis										
Bordetella										
Lyme Disease										
Rabies										
Antibody titer tests (state which tests are run)										

Notes _____

_____

_____

_____

_____

_____

Health Testing/Health History

Name _____

Date	Weight	Name of Test/Reason for Visit	Results	Veterinarian

Health Testing/Health History

Name _____

Date	Weight	Name of Test/Reason for Visit	Results	Veterinarian

Photo of My Beloved Dog

Registered Name _____ Call Name _____

Dog Information

Name _____ DOB _____

AKC# _____ Other registry # _____

Breed _____ Color/Markings _____

Sex_____DNA#_____Microchip#_____

Owner(s) _____

Contact _____

Breeder(s) _____

Contact _____

Date of Acquisition _____ Date & Duration of Lease, if any _____

Sire x Dam _____

Health, Nutrition, Routine

Medications: _____

Heartworm Medication: _____

Flea/Tick Prevention: _____

Allergies: _____

Food Brand & Type (wet and/or dry; raw and/or cooked; homemade or commercial): _____

_____

Supplements & Treats _____

Feeding Schedule: _____

Routine/Likes/Dislikes: _____

_____

Medical Insurance Policy: _____

EMERGENCY CONTACT: _____

Achievements, Memories, and Milestones

Record you dog's Champion titles, Awards and Honors, Best In Show, Certifications, training classes completed, or any achievements, memories, and milestones.

Achievement: _____ Date earned: _____

Achievement: _____ Date earned: _____

Achievement: _____ Date earned: _____

Achievement: _____ Date earned: _____

Achievement: _____ Date earned: _____

Achievement: _____ Date earned: _____

Achievement: _____ Date earned: _____

Achievement: _____ Date earned: _____

Achievement: _____ Date earned: _____

Achievement: _____ Date earned: _____

Achievement: _____ Date earned: _____

Achievement: _____ Date earned: _____

Notes _____

_____

_____

_____

_____

_____

Vaccination Record

Name _____

Age										
Date										
Distemper										
Adenovirus										
Parainfluenza										
Parvovirus										
Coronavirus										
Leptospirosis										
Bordetella										
Lyme Disease										
Rabies										
Antibody titer tests (state which tests are run)										

Notes _____

_____

_____

_____

_____

138

Health Testing/Health History

Name _____

Date	Weight	Name of Test/Reason for Visit	Results	Veterinarian

Health Testing/Health History

Name _____

Date	Weight	Name of Test/Reason for Visit	Results	Veterinarian

Conformation

What is a Conformation Show?

Dog shows, officially known as "conformation shows," are one of many competitive dog sport events that give owners and their dogs the opportunity to experience teamwork, display their dogs conformation and training, and have fun together. During a show, the dogs are being judged by pure breed experts (judges) that will look at the dog's conformation, meaning his physical characteristics, movement, and temperament, in order to determine which dogs measure up most closely to the breed standard.

The American Kennel Club states, "While they may seem glamorous, the true purpose of conformation showing is to evaluate breeding stock. The dog's conformation—his overall appearance and structure—is an indication of the dog's ability to produce quality purebred puppies, and that is what is being judged in the ring." Conformation shows are also known as All-Breed, Group, or Specialty shows.

For more information please visit www.akc.org

Everyone thinks
they have the best dog,
and none of them are wrong.
—W. R. Purche

Name of Dog: _Joyful Sir William, "Willy"_ D.O.B. _8-10-2013_ Breed: _CKCS_

Titles: _Champion, earned 8/6/2015_ Organization: _AKC_ Event: _Conformation_

	Date	Show	Judge	Class	Placement in Class	Entry in Class	Total Entry	Points	Group	BIS
1	4/10/14	Fork Ridge K.C.	Mr. George Nigard	puppy 6-9 mth	2	4	13	/		
2	5/20/15	Three Rivers Kennel Club	Mrs. Lyn Shaw	B.B.E.	1	5	8	WD 2 pt.		
3	6/10/15	Roan Valley K.C.	Dr. Gerald Tibault	Open	1	3	15	3 pt. MAJOR		
4	7/4/15	Rose Hill K.C. New York	Mr. Ryan Linford	B.B.E.	2	4	10	/		
5	7/12/15	Sage Brook K.C.	Mrs. Vivian Sylvester	Open	1	6	20	BOB 4 pt. MAJOR	4	
6	7/20/15	Nimble Rock K.C.	Mr. Howard Flanders	Open	3	4	8	/		
7	7/21/15	Horse Haven K.C.	Dr. Edward Kendal	B.B.E.	1	2	10	BOW 3 pt. MAJOR		
8	8/5/15	Skyland K.C.	Linda Lee Walters	Open	1	3	5	1 pt.		
9	8/6/15	Rockbed County Kennel Club	Mr. Morris Fitspatrick	Open	1	4	7	2 pt.		
10		New Champion!								
11										
12										
13										
14										
15										

142

Shows

Name of Dog:_____ D.O.B. _____ Breed: _____

Titles: _____ Organization:_____ Event: _____

	Date	Show	Judge	Class	Placement in Class	Entry in Class	Total Entry	Points	Group	BIS
1										
2										
3										
4										
5										
6										
7										
8										
9										
10										
11										
12										
13										
14										
15										

Notes & Comments about the Show & Judges

1 _____

_____

2 _____

_____

3 _____

_____

4 _____

_____

5 _____

_____

6 _____

_____

7 _____

_____

8 _____

_____

9 _____

_____

10 _____

_____

11 _____

_____

12 _____

_____

13 _____

_____

14 _____

_____

15 _____

_____

Shows

Name of Dog:_____ D.O.B. _____ Breed: _____

Titles: _____ Organization:_____Event: _____

	Date	Show	Judge	Class	Placement in Class	Entry in Class	Total Entry	Points	Group	BIS
1										
2										
3										
4										
5										
6										
7										
8										
9										
10										
11										
12										
13										
14										
15										

Notes & Comments about the Show & Judges

1 _____
_____

2 _____
_____

3 _____
_____

4 _____
_____

5 _____
_____

6 _____
_____

7 _____
_____

8 _____
_____

9 _____
_____

10 _____
_____

11 _____
_____

12 _____
_____

13 _____
_____

14 _____
_____

15 _____
_____

Shows

Name of Dog:_____ D.O.B. _____ Breed: _____

Titles: _____ Organization:_____ Event: _____

	Date	Show	Judge	Class	Placement in Class	Entry in Class	Total Entry	Points	Group	BIS
1										
2										
3										
4										
5										
6										
7										
8										
9										
10										
11										
12										
13										
14										
15										

Notes & Comments about the Show & Judges

1 _____
_____

2 _____
_____

3 _____
_____

4 _____
_____

5 _____
_____

6 _____
_____

7 _____
_____

8 _____
_____

9 _____
_____

10 _____
_____

11 _____
_____

12 _____
_____

13 _____
_____

14 _____
_____

15 _____
_____

Shows

Name of Dog:_____ D.O.B. _____ Breed: _____

Titles: _____ Organization:_____Event: _____

	Date	Show	Judge	Class	Placement in Class	Entry in Class	Total Entry	Points	Group	BIS
1										
2										
3										
4										
5										
6										
7										
8										
9										
10										
11										
12										
13										
14										
15										

Notes & Comments about the Show & Judges

1 _____

_____

2 _____

_____

3 _____

_____

4 _____

_____

5 _____

_____

6 _____

_____

7 _____

_____

8 _____

_____

9 _____

_____

10 _____

_____

11 _____

_____

12 _____

_____

13 _____

_____

14 _____

_____

15 _____

_____

150

Shows

Name of Dog:_____ D.O.B. _____ Breed: _____

Titles: _____ Organization:_____ Event: _____

	Date	Show	Judge	Class	Placement in Class	Entry in Class	Total Entry	Points	Group	BIS
1										
2										
3										
4										
5										
6										
7										
8										
9										
10										
11										
12										
13										
14										
15										

Notes & Comments about the Show & Judges

1 _____

_____

2 _____

_____

3 _____

_____

4 _____

_____

5 _____

_____

6 _____

_____

7 _____

_____

8 _____

_____

9 _____

_____

10 _____

_____

11 _____

_____

12 _____

_____

13 _____

_____

14 _____

_____

15 _____

_____

Shows

Name of Dog:_____ D.O.B. _____ Breed: _____

Titles: _____ Organization:_____Event: _____

	Date	Show	Judge	Class	Placement in Class	Entry in Class	Total Entry	Points	Group	BIS
1										
2										
3										
4										
5										
6										
7										
8										
9										
10										
11										
12										
13										
14										
15										

Notes & Comments about the Show & Judges

1 _____
_____

2 _____
_____

3 _____
_____

4 _____
_____

5 _____
_____

6 _____
_____

7 _____
_____

8 _____
_____

9 _____
_____

10 _____
_____

11 _____
_____

12 _____
_____

13 _____
_____

14 _____
_____

15 _____
_____

Shows

Name of Dog:_____ D.O.B. _____ Breed: _____ _____

Titles: _____ Organization:_____Event: _____

	Date	Show	Judge	Class	Placement in Class	Entry in Class	Total Entry	Points	Group	BIS
1										
2										
3										
4										
5										
6										
7										
8										
9										
10										
11										
12										
13										
14										
15										

Notes & Comments about the Show & Judges

1 _____

_____

2 _____

_____

3 _____

_____

4 _____

_____

5 _____

_____

6 _____

_____

7 _____

_____

8 _____

_____

9 _____

_____

10 _____

_____

11 _____

_____

12 _____

_____

13 _____

_____

14 _____

_____

15 _____

_____

Shows

Name of Dog:_____ D.O.B. _____ Breed: _____

Titles: _____ Organization:_____ Event: _____

	Date	Show	Judge	Class	Placement in Class	Entry in Class	Total Entry	Points	Group	BIS
1										
2										
3										
4										
5										
6										
7										
8										
9										
10										
11										
12										
13										
14										
15										

Notes & Comments about the Show & Judges

1 _____

_____

2 _____

_____

3 _____

_____

4 _____

_____

5 _____

_____

6 _____

_____

7 _____

_____

8 _____

_____

9 _____

_____

10 _____

_____

11 _____

_____

12 _____

_____

13 _____

_____

14 _____

_____

15 _____

_____

Shows

Name of Dog:_____ D.O.B. _____ Breed: _____

Titles: _____ Organization:_____ Event: _____

	Date	Show	Judge	Class	Placement in Class	Entry in Class	Total Entry	Points	Group	BIS
1										
2										
3										
4										
5										
6										
7										
8										
9										
10										
11										
12										
13										
14										
15										

1 _____
_____
2 _____
_____
3 _____
_____
4 _____
_____
5 _____
_____
6 _____
_____
7 _____
_____
8 _____
_____
9 _____
_____
10 _____
_____
11 _____
_____
12 _____
_____
13 _____
_____
14 _____
_____
15 _____
_____

Shows

Name of Dog:_____ D.O.B. _____ Breed: _____

Titles: _____ Organization:_____ Event: _____

	Date	Show	Judge	Class	Placement in Class	Entry in Class	Total Entry	Points	Group	BIS
1										
2										
3										
4										
5										
6										
7										
8										
9										
10										
11										
12										
13										
14										
15										

Notes & Comments about the Show & Judges

1 _____

_____

2 _____

_____

3 _____

_____

4 _____

_____

5 _____

_____

6 _____

_____

7 _____

_____

8 _____

_____

9 _____

_____

10 _____

_____

11 _____

_____

12 _____

_____

13 _____

_____

14 _____

_____

15 _____

_____

Shows

Name of Dog:_____ D.O.B. _____ Breed: _____

Titles: _____ Organization:_____ Event: _____

	Date	Show	Judge	Class	Placement in Class	Entry in Class	Total Entry	Points	Group	BIS
1										
2										
3										
4										
5										
6										
7										
8										
9										
10										
11										
12										
13										
14										
15										

Notes & Comments about the Show & Judges

1 _____

_____

2 _____

_____

3 _____

_____

4 _____

_____

5 _____

_____

6 _____

_____

7 _____

_____

8 _____

_____

9 _____

_____

10 _____

_____

11 _____

_____

12 _____

_____

13 _____

_____

14 _____

_____

15 _____

_____

Shows

Name of Dog:_____ D.O.B. _____ Breed: _____

Titles: _____ Organization:_____ Event: _____

	Date	Show	Judge	Class	Placement in Class	Entry in Class	Total Entry	Points	Group	BIS
1										
2										
3										
4										
5										
6										
7										
8										
9										
10										
11										
12										
13										
14										
15										

Notes & Comments about the Show & Judges

1 _____

_____

2 _____

_____

3 _____

_____

4 _____

_____

5 _____

_____

6 _____

_____

7 _____

_____

8 _____

_____

9 _____

_____

10 _____

_____

11 _____

_____

12 _____

_____

13 _____

_____

14 _____

_____

15 _____

_____

Shows

Name of Dog:_____ D.O.B. _____ Breed: _____

Titles: _____ Organization:_____ Event: _____

	Date	Show	Judge	Class	Placement in Class	Entry in Class	Total Entry	Points	Group	BIS
1										
2										
3										
4										
5										
6										
7										
8										
9										
10										
11										
12										
13										
14										
15										

Notes & Comments about the Show & Judges

1 _____

_____

2 _____

_____

3 _____

_____

4 _____

_____

5 _____

_____

6 _____

_____

7 _____

_____

8 _____

_____

9 _____

_____

10 _____

_____

11 _____

_____

12 _____

_____

13 _____

_____

14 _____

_____

15 _____

_____

Shows

Name of Dog:_____ D.O.B. _____ Breed: _____

Titles: _____ Organization:_____ Event: _____

	Date	Show	Judge	Class	Placement in Class	Entry in Class	Total Entry	Points	Group	BIS
1										
2										
3										
4										
5										
6										
7										
8										
9										
10										
11										
12										
13										
14										
15										

Notes & Comments about the Show & Judges

1 _____

_____

2 _____

_____

3 _____

_____

4 _____

_____

5 _____

_____

6 _____

_____

7 _____

_____

8 _____

_____

9 _____

_____

10 _____

_____

11 _____

_____

12 _____

_____

13 _____

_____

14 _____

_____

15 _____

_____

Shows

Name of Dog:_____ D.O.B. _____ Breed: _____

Titles: _____ Organization:_____ Event: _____

	Date	Show	Judge	Class	Placement in Class	Entry in Class	Total Entry	Points	Group	BIS
1										
2										
3										
4										
5										
6										
7										
8										
9										
10										
11										
12										
13										
14										
15										

Notes & Comments about the Show & Judges

1 _____

_____

2 _____

_____

3 _____

_____

4 _____

_____

5 _____

_____

6 _____

_____

7 _____

_____

8 _____

_____

9 _____

_____

10 _____

_____

11 _____

_____

12 _____

_____

13 _____

_____

14 _____

_____

15 _____

_____

Shows

Name of Dog:_____ D.O.B. _____ Breed: _____

Titles: _____ Organization:_____ Event: _____

	Date	Show	Judge	Class	Placement in Class	Entry in Class	Total Entry	Points	Group	BIS
1										
2										
3										
4										
5										
6										
7										
8										
9										
10										
11										
12										
13										
14										
15										

Notes & Comments about the Show & Judges

1 _____

_____

2 _____

_____

3 _____

_____

4 _____

_____

5 _____

_____

6 _____

_____

7 _____

_____

8 _____

_____

9 _____

_____

10 _____

_____

11 _____

_____

12 _____

_____

13 _____

_____

14 _____

_____

15 _____

_____

Shows

Name of Dog:_____ D.O.B. _____ Breed: _____

Titles: _____ Organization:_____ Event: _____

	Date	Show	Judge	Class	Placement in Class	Entry in Class	Total Entry	Points	Group	BIS
1										
2										
3										
4										
5										
6										
7										
8										
9										
10										
11										
12										
13										
14										
15										

Notes & Comments about the Show & Judges

1 _____

_____

2 _____

_____

3 _____

_____

4 _____

_____

5 _____

_____

6 _____

_____

7 _____

_____

8 _____

_____

9 _____

_____

10 _____

_____

11 _____

_____

12 _____

_____

13 _____

_____

14 _____

_____

15 _____

_____

Shows

Name of Dog:_____ D.O.B. _____ Breed: _____

Titles: _____ Organization:_____ Event: _____

	Date	Show	Judge	Class	Placement in Class	Entry in Class	Total Entry	Points	Group	BIS
1										
2										
3										
4										
5										
6										
7										
8										
9										
10										
11										
12										
13										
14										
15										

Notes & Comments about the Show & Judges

1 _____
_____
2 _____
_____
3 _____
_____
4 _____
_____
5 _____
_____
6 _____
_____
7 _____
_____
8 _____
_____
9 _____
_____
10 _____
_____
11 _____
_____
12 _____
_____
13 _____
_____
14 _____
_____
15 _____
_____

Shows

Name of Dog:_____ D.O.B. _____ Breed: _____

Titles: _____ Organization:_____ Event: _____

	Date	Show	Judge	Class	Placement in Class	Entry in Class	Total Entry	Points	Group	BIS
1										
2										
3										
4										
5										
6										
7										
8										
9										
10										
11										
12										
13										
14										
15										

Notes & Comments about the Show & Judges

1 _____

_____

2 _____

_____

3 _____

_____

4 _____

_____

5 _____

_____

6 _____

_____

7 _____

_____

8 _____

_____

9 _____

_____

10 _____

_____

11 _____

_____

12 _____

_____

13 _____

_____

14 _____

_____

15 _____

_____

Shows

Name of Dog:_____ D.O.B. _____ Breed: _____

Titles: _____ Organization:_____ Event: _____

	Date	Show	Judge	Class	Placement in Class	Entry in Class	Total Entry	Points	Group	BIS
1										
2										
3										
4										
5										
6										
7										
8										
9										
10										
11										
12										
13										
14										
15										

Notes & Comments about the Show & Judges

1 _____

_____

2 _____

_____

3 _____

_____

4 _____

_____

5 _____

_____

6 _____

_____

7 _____

_____

8 _____

_____

9 _____

_____

10 _____

_____

11 _____

_____

12 _____

_____

13 _____

_____

14 _____

_____

15 _____

_____

Shows

Name of Dog:_____ D.O.B. _____ Breed: _____

Titles: _____ Organization:_____ Event: _____

	Date	Show	Judge	Class	Placement in Class	Entry in Class	Total Entry	Points	Group	BIS
1										
2										
3										
4										
5										
6										
7										
8										
9										
10										
11										
12										
13										
14										
15										

Notes & Comments about the Show & Judges

1 _____
_____

2 _____
_____

3 _____
_____

4 _____
_____

5 _____
_____

6 _____
_____

7 _____
_____

8 _____
_____

9 _____
_____

10 _____
_____

11 _____
_____

12 _____
_____

13 _____
_____

14 _____
_____

15 _____
_____

Shows

Name of Dog:_____ D.O.B. _____ Breed: _____

Titles: _____ Organization:_____ Event: _____

	Date	Show	Judge	Class	Placement in Class	Entry in Class	Total Entry	Points	Group	BIS
1										
2										
3										
4										
5										
6										
7										
8										
9										
10										
11										
12										
13										
14										
15										

Notes & Comments about the Show & Judges

1 _____
_____

2 _____
_____

3 _____
_____

4 _____
_____

5 _____
_____

6 _____
_____

7 _____
_____

8 _____
_____

9 _____
_____

10 _____
_____

11 _____
_____

12 _____
_____

13 _____
_____

14 _____
_____

15 _____
_____

Shows

Name of Dog:_____ D.O.B. _____ Breed: _____

Titles: _____ Organization:_____ Event: _____

	Date	Show	Judge	Class	Placement in Class	Entry in Class	Total Entry	Points	Group	BIS
1										
2										
3										
4										
5										
6										
7										
8										
9										
10										
11										
12										
13										
14										
15										

Notes & Comments about the Show & Judges

1 _____

_____

2 _____

_____

3 _____

_____

4 _____

_____

5 _____

_____

6 _____

_____

7 _____

_____

8 _____

_____

9 _____

_____

10 _____

_____

11 _____

_____

12 _____

_____

13 _____

_____

14 _____

_____

15 _____

_____

Shows

Name of Dog:_____ D.O.B. _____ Breed: _____

Titles: _____ Organization:_____ Event: _____

	Date	Show	Judge	Class	Placement in Class	Entry in Class	Total Entry	Points	Group	BIS
1										
2										
3										
4										
5										
6										
7										
8										
9										
10										
11										
12										
13										
14										
15										

Notes & Comments about the Show & Judges

1 _____

_____

2 _____

_____

3 _____

_____

4 _____

_____

5 _____

_____

6 _____

_____

7 _____

_____

8 _____

_____

9 _____

_____

10 _____

_____

11 _____

_____

12 _____

_____

13 _____

_____

14 _____

_____

15 _____

_____

Shows

Name of Dog:_____ D.O.B. _____ Breed: _____

Titles: _____ Organization:_____ Event: _____

	Date	Show	Judge	Class	Placement in Class	Entry in Class	Total Entry	Points	Group	BIS
1										
2										
3										
4										
5										
6										
7										
8										
9										
10										
11										
12										
13										
14										
15										

Notes & Comments about the Show & Judges

1 _____

_____

2 _____

_____

3 _____

_____

4 _____

_____

5 _____

_____

6 _____

_____

7 _____

_____

8 _____

_____

9 _____

_____

10 _____

_____

11 _____

_____

12 _____

_____

13 _____

_____

14 _____

_____

15 _____

_____

Shows

Name of Dog:_____ D.O.B. _____ Breed: _____

Titles: _____ Organization:_____ Event: _____

	Date	Show	Judge	Class	Placement in Class	Entry in Class	Total Entry	Points	Group	BIS
1										
2										
3										
4										
5										
6										
7										
8										
9										
10										
11										
12										
13										
14										
15										

Notes & Comments about the Show & Judges

1 _____

_____

2 _____

_____

3 _____

_____

4 _____

_____

5 _____

_____

6 _____

_____

7 _____

_____

8 _____

_____

9 _____

_____

10 _____

_____

11 _____

_____

12 _____

_____

13 _____

_____

14 _____

_____

15 _____

_____

Shows

Name of Dog:_____ D.O.B. _____ Breed: _____

Titles: _____ Organization:_____ Event: _____

	Date	Show	Judge	Class	Placement in Class	Entry in Class	Total Entry	Points	Group	BIS
1										
2										
3										
4										
5										
6										
7										
8										
9										
10										
11										
12										
13										
14										
15										

Notes & Comments about the Show & Judges

1 _____
_____

2 _____
_____

3 _____
_____

4 _____
_____

5 _____
_____

6 _____
_____

7 _____
_____

8 _____
_____

9 _____
_____

10 _____
_____

11 _____
_____

12 _____
_____

13 _____
_____

14 _____
_____

15 _____
_____

Shows

Name of Dog:_____ D.O.B. _____ Breed: _____

Titles: _____ Organization:_____ Event: _____

	Date	Show	Judge	Class	Placement in Class	Entry in Class	Total Entry	Points	Group	BIS
1										
2										
3										
4										
5										
6										
7										
8										
9										
10										
11										
12										
13										
14										
15										

Notes & Comments about the Show & Judges

1 _____

_____

2 _____

_____

3 _____

_____

4 _____

_____

5 _____

_____

6 _____

_____

7 _____

_____

8 _____

_____

9 _____

_____

10 _____

_____

11 _____

_____

12 _____

_____

13 _____

_____

14 _____

_____

15 _____

_____

Shows

Name of Dog:_____ D.O.B. _____ Breed: _____

Titles: _____ Organization:_____ Event: _____

	Date	Show	Judge	Class	Placement in Class	Entry in Class	Total Entry	Points	Group	BIS
1										
2										
3										
4										
5										
6										
7										
8										
9										
10										
11										
12										
13										
14										
15										

Notes & Comments about the Show & Judges

1 _____

_____

2 _____

_____

3 _____

_____

4 _____

_____

5 _____

_____

6 _____

_____

7 _____

_____

8 _____

_____

9 _____

_____

10 _____

_____

11 _____

_____

12 _____

_____

13 _____

_____

14 _____

_____

15 _____

_____

Shows

Name of Dog:_____ D.O.B. _____ Breed: _____

Titles: _____ Organization:_____ Event: _____

	Date	Show	Judge	Class	Placement in Class	Entry in Class	Total Entry	Points	Group	BIS
1										
2										
3										
4										
5										
6										
7										
8										
9										
10										
11										
12										
13										
14										
15										

Notes & Comments about the Show & Judges

1 _____
_____

2 _____
_____

3 _____
_____

4 _____
_____

5 _____
_____

6 _____
_____

7 _____
_____

8 _____
_____

9 _____
_____

10 _____
_____

11 _____
_____

12 _____
_____

13 _____
_____

14 _____
_____

15 _____
_____

Shows

Name of Dog:_____ D.O.B. _____ Breed: _____

Titles: _____ Organization:_____ Event: _____

	Date	Show	Judge	Class	Placement in Class	Entry in Class	Total Entry	Points	Group	BIS
1										
2										
3										
4										
5										
6										
7										
8										
9										
10										
11										
12										
13										
14										
15										

Notes & Comments about the Show & Judges

1 _____
_____

2 _____
_____

3 _____
_____

4 _____
_____

5 _____
_____

6 _____
_____

7 _____
_____

8 _____
_____

9 _____
_____

10 _____
_____

11 _____
_____

12 _____
_____

13 _____
_____

14 _____
_____

15 _____
_____

Shows

Name of Dog:_____ D.O.B. _____ Breed: _____

Titles: _____ Organization:_____ Event: _____

	Date	Show	Judge	Class	Placement in Class	Entry in Class	Total Entry	Points	Group	BIS
1										
2										
3										
4										
5										
6										
7										
8										
9										
10										
11										
12										
13										
14										
15										

Notes & Comments about the Show & Judges

1 _____

_____

2 _____

_____

3 _____

_____

4 _____

_____

5 _____

_____

6 _____

_____

7 _____

_____

8 _____

_____

9 _____

_____

10 _____

_____

11 _____

_____

12 _____

_____

13 _____

_____

14 _____

_____

15 _____

_____

Shows

Name of Dog:_____ D.O.B. _____ Breed: _____

Titles: _____ Organization:_____ Event: _____

	Date	Show	Judge	Class	Placement in Class	Entry in Class	Total Entry	Points	Group	BIS
1										
2										
3										
4										
5										
6										
7										
8										
9										
10										
11										
12										
13										
14										
15										

Notes & Comments about the Show & Judges

1 _____

_____

2 _____

_____

3 _____

_____

4 _____

_____

5 _____

_____

6 _____

_____

7 _____

_____

8 _____

_____

9 _____

_____

10 _____

_____

11 _____

_____

12 _____

_____

13 _____

_____

14 _____

_____

15 _____

_____

Shows

Name of Dog:_____ D.O.B. _____ Breed: _____

Titles: _____ Organization:_____ Event: _____

	Date	Show	Judge	Class	Placement in Class	Entry in Class	Total Entry	Points	Group	BIS
1										
2										
3										
4										
5										
6										
7										
8										
9										
10										
11										
12										
13										
14										
15										

Notes & Comments about the Show & Judges

1 _____
_____

2 _____
_____

3 _____
_____

4 _____
_____

5 _____
_____

6 _____
_____

7 _____
_____

8 _____
_____

9 _____
_____

10 _____
_____

11 _____
_____

12 _____
_____

13 _____
_____

14 _____
_____

15 _____
_____

Shows

Name of Dog:_____ D.O.B. _____ Breed: _____

Titles: _____ Organization:_____ Event: _____

	Date	Show	Judge	Class	Placement in Class	Entry in Class	Total Entry	Points	Group	BIS
1										
2										
3										
4										
5										
6										
7										
8										
9										
10										
11										
12										
13										
14										
15										

Notes & Comments about the Show & Judges

1 _____

_____

2 _____

_____

3 _____

_____

4 _____

_____

5 _____

_____

6 _____

_____

7 _____

_____

8 _____

_____

9 _____

_____

10 _____

_____

11 _____

_____

12 _____

_____

13 _____

_____

14 _____

_____

15 _____

_____

Shows

Name of Dog:_____ D.O.B. _____ Breed: _____

Titles: _____ Organization:_____ Event: _____

	Date	Show	Judge	Class	Placement in Class	Entry in Class	Total Entry	Points	Group	BIS
1										
2										
3										
4										
5										
6										
7										
8										
9										
10										
11										
12										
13										
14										
15										

Notes & Comments about the Show & Judges

1 _____

_____

2 _____

_____

3 _____

_____

4 _____

_____

5 _____

_____

6 _____

_____

7 _____

_____

8 _____

_____

9 _____

_____

10 _____

_____

11 _____

_____

12 _____

_____

13 _____

_____

14 _____

_____

15 _____

_____

Shows

Name of Dog:_____ D.O.B. _____ Breed: _____

Titles: _____ Organization:_____ Event: _____

	Date	Show	Judge	Class	Placement in Class	Entry in Class	Total Entry	Points	Group	BIS
1										
2										
3										
4										
5										
6										
7										
8										
9										
10										
11										
12										
13										
14										
15										

Notes & Comments about the Show & Judges

1 _____
_____

2 _____
_____

3 _____
_____

4 _____
_____

5 _____
_____

6 _____
_____

7 _____
_____

8 _____
_____

9 _____
_____

10 _____
_____

11 _____
_____

12 _____
_____

13 _____
_____

14 _____
_____

15 _____
_____

Shows

Name of Dog:_____ D.O.B. _____ Breed: _____

Titles: _____ Organization:_____ Event: _____

	Date	Show	Judge	Class	Placement in Class	Entry in Class	Total Entry	Points	Group	BIS
1										
2										
3										
4										
5										
6										
7										
8										
9										
10										
11										
12										
13										
14										
15										

Notes & Comments about the Show & Judges

1 _____

_____

2 _____

_____

3 _____

_____

4 _____

_____

5 _____

_____

6 _____

_____

7 _____

_____

8 _____

_____

9 _____

_____

10 _____

_____

11 _____

_____

12 _____

_____

13 _____

_____

14 _____

_____

15 _____

_____

Shows

Name of Dog:_____ D.O.B. _____ Breed: _____

Titles: _____ Organization:_____ Event: _____

	Date	Show	Judge	Class	Placement in Class	Entry in Class	Total Entry	Points	Group	BIS
1										
2										
3										
4										
5										
6										
7										
8										
9										
10										
11										
12										
13										
14										
15										

Notes & Comments about the Show & Judges

1 _____
_____

2 _____
_____

3 _____
_____

4 _____
_____

5 _____
_____

6 _____
_____

7 _____
_____

8 _____
_____

9 _____
_____

10 _____
_____

11 _____
_____

12 _____
_____

13 _____
_____

14 _____
_____

15 _____
_____

Dog Safety Tips

Dog Safety Tips at Canine Sports Events

The safety of our dogs should be the #1 priority at all canine sports events!

- **Never leave a dog unattended in a closed car** or in direct sunlight during hot weather. The temperature inside a car is significantly higher than the temperature outside placing a dog at risk for heat stroke or possible death.

- Strenuous exercise during extremely hot days is not without risk. Make sure dogs are properly hydrated for their sports event, and resting in the shade when possible. Use crate fans, cooling mats, or an all weather SPACE blanket if needed to keep your dog cool. Don't hesitate to withdraw your dog from an event if he/she appears uncomfortable or ill.

- Wherever possible you should always avoid leaving dogs unattended in a car or RV, but if for any reason they must be left (weather permitting), do make sure to leave the car parked in a safe and shaded place. Leave the air conditioning running or the windows partially open and crate fans on to ensure proper air flow. Lock doors to prevent dog theft. Make sure your dog has access to fresh water at all times.

- Ask someone to watch your crates if you need to be absent for a moment, and/or barricade or lock crates to prevent someone from accidentally letting your dog loose.

- Be aware that leaving dogs on grooming tables or pens unattended is not without risk (i.e. falling off, jumping out).

- With a food-driven dog, be watchful that your dog doesn't snatch food from the floor or grassy areas while you are walking around together. Also, when setting up outdoors, check the grounds for foreign objects or food. There could be left over rotting bait that's infested with bugs.

- Please pick up after your dog. Have plastic bags handy to remove dogs' waste, and paper towels to wipe up any accidents indoors. Certain canine diseases can spread through fecal contact on shoes.

- Be aware of canine disease (i.e. Parvovirus) and take precautionary measures to prevent its spread. Remove and disinfect shoes and clothes when traveling to and from dog shows and other canine sports events. Stay current on vaccines.

- Make sure dogs have proper identification while traveling (i.e., collar and i.d. tag, tattoo, microchip). Collars may be removed while dogs are crated to prevent choking hazard.

- Take your dogs' health and vaccine records with you.

Being a Canine Ambassador

WE are the "official representatives" of one of the most amazing and intelligent beings on earth! As "canine ambassadors" that is our task. We are their voice. We are their guardians. It is we who plead their case and defend their cause and share with the world their incredible attributes. We also represent and uphold the future of canine sports, and people are watching. How will we handle that responsibility? What will we say when asked to share about our specific breed, dogs in general, or the sport that has captivated our attention?

Here are a few tips to help you stay focused and positive while interacting with the public.

🐾 When instructing the public on proper dog show etiquette, be gracious and kind. Most people are not aware of proper etiquette when approaching a strange dog or exhibitor at a canine sports event.

🐾 Kindly instruct people to "ask" before petting your dog or giving a treat. Explain that some dogs have special dietary needs or have sensitive stomachs. It could also be an opportune moment to instruct a child on the proper way to approach a dog.

🐾 The ask-before-petting rule also applies to touching a dog through a crate or while in a pen. If a spectator tries to touch a dog through a crate, politely advise them not to do that. Use the opportunity to explain that it is a dog's personal space and time to rest. You can also mention that some dogs (even friendly ones) may nip fingers depending on the circumstances and how they're approached.

🐾 If someone would like to speak to you during a competitive event, and you are busy preparing, kindly ask them to wait until you're finished and let them know when/if you'll be available.

🐾 Refer people to the AKC web site. The American Kennel Club Public Education department offers numerous resources to help educate children and adults about the wonderful world of dogs. Brochures, books, educational kits and fliers with popular responsible dog ownership messages, games and activities are available upon request or online at http://www.akc.org/public-education/resources/ The AKC also offers an official Canine Ambassador program for those interested in making presentations to groups of children in classrooms and other venues.

It's not always easy to focus on a competition, our dogs, and the public. But when possible, take the time to talk with spectators and allow them interact with your dogs. It's a wonderful opportunity to educate people about your breed, responsible dog ownership, the benefits of training, responsible breeding, and the wonderful qualities of purebred dogs. The future of canine sport and the well being of our beloved breed is in our hands. May passion, purpose, and love for our dogs shine through in all we do!

The Magic Number

LIVING IN A MULTI-DOG HOUSEHOLD

During dinner one evening with a respected breeder and friend, a question arose as to our "Magic Number." Without further explanation I knew immediately what he was talking about: the number of dogs we all felt comfortable living with. Years ago, when I acquired my first Cavalier King Charles Spaniel, I had no idea they'd become addictive. They're so friendly, comforting and easy to care for . . . what's one more? However as time went on, I soon realized that numbers do matter, and as my friend at dinner pointed out, "If I cross that line in the number of dogs I keep, it no longer becomes fun." That's when, in my opinion, the magic begins to fade.

In preparing this article I was pleasantly surprised to find that Cindy, my avid gardening friend, also had a "magic number." Cindy's garden could be compared to Monet's—it's extraordinarily beautiful and harmonious. People often wonder why she would want such a large garden—I mean the more you plant, the more you have to care for, right? Her response echoed the words of my heart: "It's my passion!" Cindy and I agree—we passionately love what we do, and we have the time and energy to do it. That said, we must continually reflect on our goals, making sure that we've not taken on more than we can handle. Benjamin Franklin writes, "If passion drives you, let reason be your reins."

Keep in mind that not everyone will agree on the magic number. The number five or ten might feel like pure chaos to one person and pure joy to another. Some folks aren't bothered by the endless fur on the sofa or wild games of doggie chase around the kitchen island. Some people can multi-task several litters, raise children, and manage life's activities while everyone is happy and well cared for. Others may find this impossible. We all have different time schedules, talents, abilities, and finances. I don't think it's beneficial to compare or critique each other's "garden." Rather, we should focus on our own garden and goals and work towards harmony within our home. My personal goal is to see each member of my family happy and content—husband, children, and dogs, including myself. I've learned the joy of juggling! Years ago I heard this phrase that challenged my goals: "Too many flowers in a garden and none come to bloom." I asked Cindy if this was accurate. She said it's not about "how many" seeds you plant (within reason of course), it's about making sure each seed has its own space to grow. When seeds are scattered on the ground too close together, they'll be either too tall, or too skinny, and some may even die. Her words, "It will be an ugly garden; it all depends what you want."

So I ask: do my dogs have enough space, soil, and nutrients to encourage proper growth? Making "space" for each seed can mean different things. For me it involves allotting time for individual bonding with each dog—cuddle time, training, individual grooming, daily walks and sunshine, good nutrition, and lots of TLC. It also involves working with all the dogs together to encourage group unity and focus, and my role as leader. Making "space" for our precious seedlings to thrive is definitely an all-consuming task, and if we are not careful, we can easily become overwhelmed. That's when feelings of resentment may creep in and steal our joy, and maybe even our health. Dear friend, we all need proper nutrients and space to thrive, not just our dogs. Please take care of yourselves too. Dog ownership, like gardening, should remain a joy, and seeing our garden in full bloom our greatest reward!

So what is your magic number? If you're not sure, take some time and sit with your dogs, observe how they're growing, interacting, and playing . . . Surely they will reveal the answer.

PHONE/ADDRESS BOOK

Veterinary Specialists, Pet Sitters, and Emergency Contacts

Name _____

Telephone _____ E-mail_____

Address_____

Name _____

Telephone _____ E-mail_____

Address_____

Name _____

Telephone _____ E-mail_____

Address_____

Name _____

Telephone _____ E-mail_____

Address_____

Name _____

Telephone _____ E-mail_____

Address_____

Name _____

Telephone _____ E-mail_____

Address_____

Name _____

Telephone _____ E-mail_____

Address_____

Name _____

Telephone _____ E-mail_____

Address_____

PHONE/ADDRESS BOOK

Veterinary Specialists, Pet Sitters, and Emergency Contacts

Name_____

Telephone _____ E-mail_____

Address_____

Name_____

Telephone _____ E-mail_____

Address_____

Name_____

Telephone _____ E-mail_____

Address_____

Name_____

Telephone _____ E-mail_____

Address_____

Name_____

Telephone _____ E-mail_____

Address_____

Name_____

Telephone _____ E-mail_____

Address_____

Online Shopping Sites:

_____

_____

_____

_____

_____

_____

RECOMMENDED RESOURCES

Recommended Reading

The Complete Dog Book, 20th Edition, by the American Kennel Club

The Absolute Beginners Guide to Showing Your Dogs, by Cheryl S. Smith

Born To Win: Breed To Succeed, second edition, by Patricia Craige Trotter

K-9 Structure & Terminology, by Edward M. Gilbert, Jr. and Thelma R. Brown

The Dog in Action: A Study of Anatomy and Locomotion as Applying to all Breeds, by McDowell Lyon

Dog Steps, A New Look, by Rachel Page Elliot

Feeling Outnumbered? How to Manage and Enjoy Your Multi-dog Household, 2nd edition, by Karen B. London, Ph.D. and Patricia B. McConnell, Ph.D.

The Book of the Bitch, A Complete Guide to Understanding and Caring for Bitches, by J.M. Evans and Kay White

Canine Reproduction: The Breeder's Guide, 3rd edition, by Phyllis A. Holst

A Breeder's Companion, Record Keeping for Your Dogs' Litters, by Leila Grandemange

Useful Web Links

- AKC Canine Health Foundation: www.akcchf.org

- OFA, Orthopedic Foundation for Animals: www.offa.org

- Health Testing Requirements: www.akc.org/dog-breeders/bred-with-heart/health-testing-requirements/

- Canine Health Information Center (CHIC): http://caninehealthinfo.org/

- Breed Specific Training and General Care: www.akc.org/events/training-clubs/

- A Guide To Responsible Breeding: www.akc.org/dog-breeders/responsible-breeding/

- The American Animal Hospital Association: www.aaha.org

- Dr. Jean Dodds' Pet Health Resource Blog: www.hemopet.org

- Public Education Resources: www.akc.org/public-education/

- The United States Dog Agility Association: www.usdaa.com

- AKC registered handlers program: www.akc.org/events/handlers/

- AKC Events: conformation, agility, obedience, rally, etc.: www.akc.org/events/

ORDER INFORMATION

Please visit
www.SunnyvillePublishing.com

> He is your friend, your partner,
> your defender, your dog.
> You are his life, his love, his leader.
> He will be yours, faithful and true,
> to the last beat of his heart.
> You owe it to him
> to be worthy of such devotion.
>
> —Unknown

Special Thanks

Sincere thanks to the veterinarians and to the long time breeder friends and judges who shared their expertise while I was writing this book; ED&M Design; my precious family; and of course God, who makes all things possible!

Photo Credits: all photos by Leila Grandemange of her and her dogs, except as noted:
p. 5 Boxer: Maura McIntosh and her dog Keeva
p. 5 agility photo: Ellie Allen Cook
p. 140 dog jumping: Shelly Fields Photography Studio, Rachel Venier and her dog Devon
p. 140 dog show: MorgueFile.com
p. 221 German Shepherds: Ruperon Shepherds, Ruth Fisher
p. 225 Labrador Retrievers: istockphoto.com ©lizcen photo:59051058

CPSIA information can be obtained at www.ICGtesting.com
Printed in the USA
BVOW04s1654030915

415491BV00004B/24/P